Fossil Wings

poems by

Beverly Blatner Bagelman

Finishing Line Press
Georgetown, Kentucky

Fossil Wings

For Mom: a most formidable muse.
For my brother Jim: these wings are yours.

Copyright © 2023 by Beverly Blatner Bagelman
ISBN 979-8-88838-165-6 First Edition
All rights reserved under International and Pan-American Copyright Conventions. No part of this book may be reproduced in any manner whatsoever without written permission from the publisher, except in the case of brief quotations embodied in critical articles and reviews.

Acknowledgments

"The Gulf Coast is a Southern Baptist Preacher" first appeared in the Spring 2021 edition of *Ocotillo Review*.

I am grateful to my daughter Mallary Staney, a perpetual source of inspiration and joy, whose ability to penetrate to the core truth of a matter helped me transform some pretty rough pieces. My husband Gary, the ground to my sky, whose love and multifaceted support provided space and time for me to pursue this passion.

Appreciation to: Nicole Spradling, friend and fellow writer for her encouragement, support, and enthusiasm. Charlotte Gullick, a gifted teacher, writer, and nurturer of this writer's soul. Brian Cutean, a rare and true lifelong creative, and the first friend to call me "a poet."

Special thanks to Austin Poetry Society, and APS critique group's Beth Kropf's commitment to the craft of fellow poets. Joy Harjo, a mentor both on the page and in my dreams who has unknowingly kept me on track. To all the teachers of craft whose articles, books, and virtual classes have made a huge difference in this emerging writer's journey. To CMG, whose generosity, patience and persistent prodding made this possible. Thank you all for sharing so generously your hard-earned wisdom.

With special gratitude to my younger sister, who made me believe, long ago, I had something worth saying.

Publisher: Leah Huete de Maines
Editor: Christen Kincaid
Cover Art: Beverly Blatner Bagelman
Author Photo: William C. Staney
Cover Design: Elizabeth Maines McCleavy

Order online: www.finishinglinepress.com
also available on amazon.com

Author inquiries and mail orders:
Finishing Line Press
PO Box 1626
Georgetown, Kentucky 40324
USA

Table of Contents

Part One: Geode
Geode 1
Painted Desert 2
Blind Spot 3
Not About the Chanterelles 4
Rocking Chair 5
Her House 6
Delayed Flight 7

Part Two: Iridescent Scar
Iridescent Scar 9
Repossession 1960 10
Repossession 1960 Part 2 11
Dressed in Yellow 12
Brother's Storm 14
Crimson Flurry 15
Tornado 1940 16
Tornado 1940: What Happened Next 17
After the Storm 18
Lasius Niger 19
Oil Refinery Takes Over Childhood Neighborhood 20
Shifting Wind 21
Don't Waste Your Bullets 22
Gulf Coast is a Southern Baptist Preacher 23
Tide at Perigee 24

Part Three: Fossil Wings
Pantoum for Loss 25
Black Exodus 26
Zebras on Lake Travis, Texas 27
Pocket Protector 28
Chain Stitch 29
Permanent Marker 30
The Dock 31
The Mind as Archaeological Site 32
Axis Ballroom 33
Fossil Wings 34

Part One: Geode

Geode

small moon of rust and grey
remnant of turbulent past
when earth rumbled and roared
poured ember rivers
down its face

over time it cools, cracks, slows
imprints its memories
in clay shadows
where it lay for millions of years

without being prodded
so I tap gently
to open the wound

when it cracks
an ancient tomb
of quartz arises
brilliant and clear

Part One: Geode

Painted Desert

The peach and plum sands were dark
under the waning moon when my dad
pulled into the rest stop.

Everyone else asleep, I slipped through
the camper, shutting the door behind me softly.

I crossed the barren parking lot where my dad
stood in the yellow lamplight, comparing
his folded map to the fogged plexiglass directory.

When I entered the bathroom, the steel door
slammed, bouncing off the cement walls.
The faucet coughed and spat resentfully.

Outside, my dad sat on a stone bench
smoking a cigarette. He faced the moon
that lay atop a dark mesa, a giant
sliver of coconut.

He gave me a quarter to feed a
cantankerous looking machine.
It lumbered noisily, delivering the frosty soda.

I sat beside him, sipping the orange can.
The darkness bubbling over the plateau,
the peaches, plums and camper sleeping.

Part One: Geode

Blind Spot

It was a card game we played on the porch.
She was 9 or 10, and I was a young mother,
trying too hard to be a good one.

We'd draw a card without looking,
hold it on the forehead facing out, guess
whose card was higher than the other,
then place our bets.

We learn early to define ourselves
by looking outward; to assay the atmosphere
of other worlds, as we comprehend our own.

Am I good enough? I looked at her.
High grades, manners, constrained behavior.
Was she good enough? She looked at me.

We sat, circling the other, as dogs barked,
doors slammed, children played.

Finally, a neighbor walking by with her beagle,
stopped and smiled as if she knew the game.
"Challenging," she said.

From a distance it's easy to see the invisible
force of rotating objects. We finally called
a truce, tossed our cards down, and
discovered we both had 7s.

She arched her eyebrows in that crooked
question mark of surprise I always loved
as we both laughed and gathered the cards.

By this time, the moths were gathering around
the blue flicker of the streetlight, and Saturn and Venus
had begun their arc across the western sky.

Part One: Geode

Not About the Chanterelles

It wasn't the way the west desert wind stained the clouds red,
or how the rust-colored rain hammered the car, blotting out the terrain.

Or when two ancient pumps finally appeared on the plains,
how my daughter and I scoured the car for loose change.

And later, when we discussed the divorce, it wasn't how
the eight-year-old unleashed like a storm.

And when I fumbled for something to say, it wasn't the cliche
I offered, thin as a rain poncho, for support.

But there was something about my daughter as she slept:
her fingers like loose woven straw on her lap,
her hair coiling and meandering across the flattened seat,
that made me stop, beside a swamped patch of chanterelles, to think.

There was a cowbird needling for mites on the haunches of a Hereford.
But it was the cow, how it stood unflinching in the punishing rain,
that made me realize how poorly I'd prepared us for this terrain.

It was about my urge to trample the muddy field and rattle the cow.
It was about my yearning to wrap us both in its hide.

PART ONE: GEODE

Rocking Chair

Rock and creak
and rock and creak.

On mother's lap
we drift to sleep.

Her steady heart
a steady beat.

We feel her breast
against our cheek.

The world stands still
outside the door.

We rock and creak
against the floor.

Part One: Geode

Her House

One desk, two roller chairs,
twelve hospital discharge folders.

Washed plates on counter
mail stacks in cupboard,
four types of Little Debbie,
two opened Pringles, three unopened.

Wicker basket, unfolded laundry-clean.
Metal pill safe, locked.
Three new lip sticks, mascara, one blond wig.
Twenty-one oxygen tanks, some full.

Oil paints, canvass, brushes,
one half an abstract horse.

A bulletin board with a picture of us as teens:
Two sisters at the beach
one crazy summer.

A metal-railed bed where she writes
a grocery list. A one-of-a
kind, still infinitely persuasive
rose-tinted smile;

"Do you mind? I only need a couple of things."

Part One: Geode

Delayed Flight

She flipped up blankets,
stooped under beds, rifled through
closets as I followed behind,
my own panic rising.

But when she turned to face me
something was different.
Her back was runway straight,
her cheeks flushed.

I pressed her hand into mine and told
her not to worry, she didn't
need the oxygen mask anymore.

But she'd already begun to dissolve
in despair, slipping through my fingers
like dishwater in a basin.

I gripped her sleeves, and lifted
until my eyes aligned with the
umbrous region of her face.

"You're okay, sis." I insisted.

She remained opaque, as if
suspicious of how I could know this.

How did I know this?

Then a realization flashed
"You died!" followed by
an explosion of lucidity,
"You're not suffering anymore!"

The force of this awareness
dissolved the curtains, roof,
walls, even scrubbed the atmosphere
of clouds so that we stood bare skinned
against black ice. I recognized three

Part One: Geode

pulsing orbs from different
constellations and opened my mouth
to say their names, but she was waiting
for me, two sparks grounded, as if I held
her final boarding pass.

"It's alright, sis, you can go." I said,
but it wasn't until I promised I'd be okay
that the sparks ignited, coalesced, blasted up and away.

It's strange, but I don't remember which
constellation I saw her in last
even though I stayed

until each vertebrae
along her silver tail
dissolved and
fell away.

Part Two: Iridescent Scar

Iridescent Scar:
    To My Nineteen-Year-Old Self:

Three months after the accident
the bone between L3 and L4
is finally fused, so you loosen
the steel ribbed corset,
dump the back brace for good.

But a thin scar remains
on your face, carving a fault line
through your self-image.

You don't yet realize that soft pink
tissue and mended bone
are the same kind of miracle,
that scars are only laugh lines in waiting.

That the universe is made from
ruptures, liquid fire,
and bodies colliding.

So let the world come for you.
Let it break you open.

You've only to bend
like an arc of light
across your beautiful wreckage.

Part Two: Iridescent Scar

Repossession 1960

The silence jostled her awake.
Not the usual thin pitched cry but its
absence, that jolted her out of bed, down
the hall, to the baby's room.

Where behind the spindled bars
of the crib she found his plump limbs
still as stone his skin tinged ethereal blue.

She pressed him against her chest, clapped
his back with her palm, then laid
him on the braided rug, forcing
air into his little sacs until they rose
on their own, pressing thumbs
into his chest until it finally thumped back.

He would do that again.
Grow still and inanimate as if
being carried away beneath the stadium
lights of another world.

And each time she'd wrestle
him back, grip him in steel arms
as if daring the universe

To just try
and repossess
its cosmic fumble.

Part Two: Iridescent Scar

Repossession 1960, Part 2

With bundled baby in tow, she
searched the region for answers.

But when the doctors saw the purple
thumb prints on the baby's chest
they questioned his mother instead.

It wasn't until the husband
witnessed the blue blanket
of silence, as the baby clutched
then dropped his rattle,
and confirmed the incidents
in a low, measured voice,
that help was prescribed.

Large oval pills of phenobarbital
that the mother crushed
and fed to the baby
with his milk.

Part Two: Iridescent Scar

Dressed In Yellow

*Cinderella dressed in yellow
went upstairs to kiss a fellow.
Made a mistake and kissed a snake,
How many doctors would it take?*

When my brother was almost five and I was almost four, he climbed onto the kitchen counter, atop the white porcelain fridge, and pulled two small bottles from the overhead cabinet. I sat on the green tiled floor with a picture book of Cinderella.

He kept the pink pills, handed me the white ones, and said "Eat them."

When I asked why, he climbed back up, and spread his arms like wings. "Because they will make you fly! Really, Bev. Way high—in the sky."

It could've been the light from the window that made the white hairs on his arms look like tiny feathers, but I really believed he could fly right then.

"But he wasn't even five years old," said a woman in a writing class. "How did he think that pills would make him fly?"

Maybe it was something he saw on TV. Or maybe the phenobarbital prescribed for his blue baby incidents had triggered something. Or maybe he was just pre-wired that way.

But whenever the incident was mentioned growing up, it was always in a half-joking way, like the time he tried to flush me down the toilet. A little boy trying to eliminate his little sibling rival.

It was much later, at my parent's house in Tucson, I finally asked about it. It could've been the red wine, or the desert moon rippling off the pool. But I asked my mother what I'd always wondered.

"Why did I do it mom? Why did I eat that whole bottle? Those white aspirin taste so nasty!"

Mom rubbed the rim of her wine glass, then looked up at me, "Because you loved him. You would've done whatever he told you."

Part Two: Iridescent Scar

For mom, it was simple. Cinderella went upstairs because she loved the fellow. The snake is an anomaly in the story, something unforeseen.

But what if Cinderella knew about the snake, and went up there anyway? What if she knew the fellow was afraid?

It could've been how my brother took my arm as I got up to go tell mom and the yellow flecks in his eyes when he said, "Bev, don't go. Please don't leave me."

"How could you remember all that when you were so little?" the lady wondered.

Maybe it was the clicking heels as the kitchen doors swung open, the dialing phone, or my mom's voice cutting through the gathering clouds with something like, "Yes, we need a doctor. How many doctors will it take?"

Maybe it was the dry metallic mush as the words molded on my tongue.

I made a mistake.
I made a mistake.
I kissed a snake.

Part Two: Iridescent Scar

Brother's Storm

It could happen anytime, racing
matchbox cars or wheelie popping
banana seat bikes, a storm would blow
from nowhere, and take him to the ground.

I would stand, still as stone, as he
bended in its grasp: Torso arching,
arms and legs bending,
fern eyes vacant.

An electrical storm, they told us.
A seizure. We were so close
that I could feel the heat rise
from the cotton on his head.
But he was suddenly so far away.

In those days I was still following him
everywhere. If I'd had a kite
I would've held it tight
and flown across his dangerous sky.

Part Two: Iridescent Scar

Crimson Flurry

The chant pricked like a burr
in my shoe as we jumped rope at recess.

"My momma, your momma, hanging out clothes.
My momma gave your momma a bloody nose.
What color was the blood?"

I didn't care about the color.
It was the "why" of things that intrigued me, not the "what."

Why did the mothers quarrel?
Was it a grudge—a cloud of gnats hovering,
darting in and out, as they swatted and pinned?

Or was it one tiny fly of annoyance buzzing louder
and louder down the towel line, until finally
squashed in a crimson flurry near the jeans?

I knew how one thing could lead to another.
How clouds could roll across the plains, carrying
dust and soot from the panhandle and the local plant
how white diapers could turn grey as they hung on the line.

How a mother's worry lines could grow deep
as a baby sister coughed, then wheezed.
And the long nights of rocking chairs
and cool rags on hot cheeks.

I saw the chrome-sided beds where white clad
doctors sat with clipboards, asking more questions
that seemed pointless, at least to me.

The chant bothered me, because even
as the clouds grew dark, we jumped,
followed the rhythmic rounding of the rope,
never stopping to ask why.

Part Two: Iridescent Scar

Tornado 1940

My mother is five years old,
pushing her sister in a backyard swing.
In the clouds, a dark body is weaving,
bending through the sky.

It starts to skip across rooftops, spinning,
growing heavy.

Soon, it is bumping into houses, breaking windows,
tripping over tractors in the yard.

The black skirt, bedazzled with glass and metal bits,
twirls closer, starts to whine, then screech.

In the kitchen, my grandmother is frying chicken.
The stove shakes, splatters grease to the floor.

She pulls her daughters to the bathroom,
they huddle, walls rattling, shaking,
chicken still popping on the stove.

Part Two: Iridescent Scar

Tornado 1940: What Happened Next

I could've ended the story there.

A mother's wing wrapped around
her terrified starlings. She could've lighted
in the reader's mind as protector,
archetypal Madonna of sorts.

But the same wind that rattled the stove
also shattered the window above it,
blowing the curtains into
the flame, setting the walls ablaze.

My grandmother's actions
after the house burned down,
probably depict a more accurate picture:

How she packed up her daughters
along with a few donations,
dropped them off with relatives
as she set off to look for
husband number three or four.

Even the most self-serving mother
has moments of selflessness.
My grandmother was only 16
when my mother was born.

But poets and scribes are often compelled
to delineate a particular heroine
within their stories.

So I cast these lines to retrieve
my mother from her mother's shadow,
repositioning her in that light.

Part Two: Iridescent Scar

After the Storm

Leveled the house
and stripped
away the constructs
of self-identity,
I saw how the wind
had strewn the
pages of my past
across the grassy field
to flutter like flags
and the walls
were no longer walls
separating myself
from all other things
and I saw how the sun,
all along the sun
had poured everything
it had into me,
had been throwing me
balls of color
inviting me to play.

Part Two: Iridescent Scar

Lasius Niger

In the heat of long afternoons,
I punted the sides off round mounds,
as black seeds swirled in a flurry of chaos.

It wasn't the disruption I was after.
Or the dark streams of cohesion
as the ants rebuilt their domain.

It was the secret imprint on
tiny grains that intrigued me.
I was trying to understand my father.

Head down all day at work then home,
head down again, behind newspaper, as if
decoding encrypted military commands.

I am sure he would've talked to me
about my problems if he could,
but he wasn't designed that way.

He was constructed to meet the millions
of tiny needs rising from the center of the dirt hill.

He was built to carry 30 times his own body weight.

PART TWO: IRIDESCENT SCAR

Oil Refinery Takes Over Childhood Neighborhood

It was a land where metal
towers sprang from the ground
like alien beanstalks, where white
workers lived in company houses
and black workers (if any)
lived in "black town," a place
where benzene emissions
and carbon monoxide (if any)
drifted over black town first.

A place where a defiant patch of green
wedged itself between the refinery
and the white houses, a small park
with a tall steel slide that shot
us out like bb's, and an ocean wave,
part swing part merry-go-round,
that hung from heavy chains and flung
about like a storm cast ship.

This was where we padded through
thick bladed grasses, sucked honeysuckle stems,
climbed the huckleberry tree to spy
tall gas flares that stood around the plant
like giant birthday candles.

Part Two: Iridescent Scar

Shifting Wind

I feel his gaze on me
outside the small-town store.
A tall boy, older, maybe 14.
I brush dirt off my knobby knees,
rumple a paper bag,
shove change into my shorts pocket.

His dark eyes land on mine
in a way I don't quite recognize,
but they spark something beautiful,
combustible, dangerous.

I straddle my bike, flip
sun-streaked hair behind shoulders,
pop a Sweet Tart in my mouth.

My brother and his friends,
slipped off toward the football field
so I pedal off to catch them.

It is then I felt the wind behind me
the grassy scent of an oncoming storm
and my grip on the handlebars.

Part Two: Iridescent Scar

Don't Waste Your Bullets

The neighbor boys showed up
as the porch lights flicked on, slapping
rolled newspaper against open palm.
You better run! I'm playing for keeps this time.
Then thwack-smack!
Rising welts on thighs and back.

It was the orange glow of the street-light
that did it, made the boys throw harder,
the girl's bruise deeper.

But one day it stung so hot,
I did the only thing I could.

I closed my eyes until I felt a prickle
spread across my torso,
saw the tiny sprigs of down
sprout from my arms.

I stretched my wings and let a breeze
lift me above the paper missiles, flapped
my feathers in the golden wash of lamp light.

"Don't waste your bullets!" I roared.

I'd found something else to do on summer evenings.
Some would throw the paper. Some would read the paper.

But I would transform paper.
Spread it flat across my desk
and let fly
the wild dark flocks
of a young girl's mind.

Part Two: Iridescent Scar

The Gulf Coast is a Southern Baptist Preacher

It gesticulates, smacks the shore like a Bible
as sea salt stings and dunes fling
tissues to the wind.

A boy lifts a little girl under arm pits,
lunges her into the widening mouth of a brown wave.
It swallows her whole.

I think of Brother Bobby, Old Ocean TX, 1971,
our robe sleeves floating like silver wings
in the sanctuary pool.

He braced my head with one hand,
blocked my nose with the other,
then swoosh! Deep into
the pool's belly I plunged.

We were all sinners.
Even the brand-new baby
is born chock-full of guilt
by nature of its humanity.

You had to believe this to be saved
so we all believed it. Well, not
everyone believed, I guess.

Near shore the little girl emerges:
face slick with relief, eyes blinking.
She is a slightly changed girl,
who sees a slightly changed world.

Up shore a jellyfish is stranded, its tentacles
waving, prismatic in the sun.
The tide moves in, slips beneath it.
Without fanfare it is saved.

Part Two: Iridescent Scar

Tide at Perigee

The tide bled past the salt line border,
over rusty cans and plastic pails,
rose along the powdered dunes
dissolved into the clumps of sea oats.

This is where I found my brother.
Sun-streaked hair, face and shoulders
terra-cotta red, clutching the coins
our mom buried in the shallow mounds.

He'd dug that day until he'd found the cache,
then stood there basking in his win.
Even now, this is how I see him:
outlined in gold, the whole world captured in his hand.

But there are forces that pull the planet.
Moons that orchestrate the tide.
There are people that try to stop this
as if our will or love sufficed.

Tonight, the moon removes the cover,
reveals the naked coastal hide.

Perhaps I never knew my brother.
Was he a priceless ore,
or penny cast aside?

I just know I really miss him,
this empty chest now in my soul.

The moon so close I hear it whisper,

I know, sis, I know.

Part Three: Fossil Wings

Pantoum for Loss

She was moon milk and steel vine,
easy as a paper fan, intricate as origami.
Everything you'd expect, if you expected everything,
a wound stitcher, wing mender.

Easy as a paper fan, intricate as origami,
a mother fit for Eve, if Eve had a mother.
Wound stitcher, wing mender,
abhorred ornamental fruit trees.

A mother fit for Eve, if Eve had a mother,
she'd tell her, "Honey, don't blame yourself."
Abhorred ornamental fruit trees
said, "They help nobody, all for show."

Would've told me, "Honey don't blame yourself,"
as I sit now, with the silent machines
helping nobody, all for show,
as you might imagine, a hard act to follow.

I sit in her room with the silent machines.
She was moon milk, steel vine.
As you might imagine, a hard act to follow.
Everything you'd expect, if you expected everything.

Part Three: Fossil Wings

Black Exodus

You ask what to keep,
to burn, to throw away.

Had a tangible red-blue
blaze scorched the house,
it might've been easier than
the toxic mold invasion that waged
its silent war after the flooding.

You stay home, manning the frontline.
I head west to dry skies,
black mold in my blood.

What to keep: The pearl handled comb
from my mom? I must think. Justify.
The needle-point flower my young daughter made?
You must detox, store, or sacrifice.

I drive until the ocean's steel rings against
tumbled stone, then shift north up a pin-thin
road weaving through the redwoods.

How many stones can we carry?
Which are the weevils that bore silent holes
until our feed sacks are empty?

How much proof that a life was lived?
The ground rises steadily, thins
the air and grass. I think I have driven
onto another planet. A blue glow spreads
across limestone. The moon is so round and close
I could float up and touch it.

Part Three: Fossil Wings

Zebras on Lake Travis, Texas

After the last rare rain, I scan the water's edge
for arthropods or arrowheads.
But Zebra mussels span the rocks,
weave like macrame beneath the dock.

I recall the basic knots my mother taught one summer
where the river ran swift and cool.
But here the mussels wrap boat hulls,
choke motors and water lines.

With their tiny threads waving, to feed
on fish debris it's hard to believe they disrupt
food chains, exile native birds and fishes.

In the cove below, a ponderous sunfish lolls,
brandishing an orange fin. Up shore an egret
plods, plucking minnows with a tweezered beak.

I recall the wriggling crabs we trapped
and boiled in salted water. When I finally made
her bisque by heart, she'd said, "Okay,
I guess I can go now. That's all I got.'"

I didn't catch the undertones of being displaced
or recognize the notes of pride and sadness on a
mother's face. I was too young, too hungry back then.

She would've loved the arrowhead I found here
last summer, knapped from the Tonkawa, I believe,
back when the land was wild before this man-made lake.

Had they called themselves "the most human humans?"
Or was that a mistranslation? Their language,
like their land, dissected and dammed, until
a sole member buried the remains with his own hands.

As clouds gather for the next rare rain, I climb the stairs
for home when a pain shoots through my knee.
The translation reads: *I too will be replaced.*

Part Three: Fossil Wings

Pocket Protector

I pull the handkerchief from
a zippered bag and find beneath
the wafts of laundry soap,
the scent of him: sesame oil,
bourbon, something like warm tar.

He kept it stacked in a shallow
dresser drawer next to his pocket
protector: a white plastic glove
I think of often. My mom might've
given it to any one of us.

But I do have other things from him:
a slide rule with worn leather sleeve,
a rusty engineer paper stamper,
and this handkerchief.

The pocket protector held
a silver pen, its mechanical
pencil twin, a thin screwdriver,
and a tire gauge. Each item
securely clamped in place.

My dad was the protector's protector.
Without his hand and daily regimen
any one of us could've lost our way back then,
to fall into some dark recess
or random drawer.

PART THREE: FOSSIL WINGS

Chain Stitch

Around dish towels we stitched plum petals:
Grew verdant vines down denim seams, brought
rainbows up from chambray pockets. My mom
taught us to pull thread through pale cloth:
To pierce the world with color. We'd gather

around the table with friends from down
the street, wad up newspapers, pull strips
through bowls of flour paste, then wrap

around, pressing down bubbles
and lumps as we went. Mistakes didn't
upset us. We knew through accidents
our finest creations were made.

On some school days she'd work around
the clock; emerge with tweed coat with burgundy
faux fur collar, or tiny down pillows and satin
blankets for dolls. Or she'd transform beat- up
coffee tables through the miracle of decoupage.
Her fingers, strong and round, bore
down into ideas and fossilized them.

Up on this shelf, I keep the quilts that passed
through my mother to me. Around the squares
are tiny blue and red flowers. Down the sides
yellow flags and dogs. My mom's grandmother
would cut up feed sacks for dresses, then cut apart
old dresses for quilts. Throughout the blanket,
my great-grandmother mingled, diverged,
and connected patterns.

Around the border a blue thread travels, pressing
down into the batting. If you look close
you see how strong the cord, how unstoppable
the force that passes through this line.

Part Three: Fossil Wings

Permanent Marker

Here, the long-lashed
blue-eyed grass
bats and sways
in a quiet wind.

The blood-red
Indian paintbrush
punctures the air
with pointed beauty.

Everywhere garden
perennials, mad dazzle
of daffodils, purply proud
with sturdy stalks. Yellow
trumpet vines blasting.

Spring found its way this year
without a mother to cajole it
over the grey rocks of winter.

How does the lantana turn
lavender without excitement
pouring over each bloom?

My mother's half-full cup bubbled over,
spilling itself over everything.

Part Three: Fossil Wings

The Dock

For four days, pea-sized pellets
pelted the world. Puddles now
ponds, and rocky hills, rivulets.

Through shivering sheets
we press toward the dock.

A black-bellied whistler floats
behind a veil of lake weed.
Two nestlings sit, feathers
slick as polished stone.

The dock, tethered by steel cables
to the lake floor, strains and grinds
as water rises.

We wade through water-weeds,
skim over soaked planks,
crank the rusty spool handle,
loosen the leash.

The dock reels back as it heaves,
wobbles, and splashes back
down to the lake surface.

We all rise and fall
with the storm now.
Like wood-ducks, unruffled.

Part Three: Fossil Wings

The Mind as Archaeological Site

I took a pick-axe to excavate artifacts, but on the first swing,
an early memory crumbled on impact, a plush pond,
a picnic with family.

I found the oak tree with its hundreds of meandering limbs,
had stiffened like a stegosaurus spine.

And the little dark ones, the small
traumas I'd buried deep, got provoked
by the jostling soil and rose, charging
me like a sounder of wild boar.

I tended the gravesites. Dug gorges to redirect flash floods.
I stacked walls of limestone to protect against the wind.

I raked and hoed the surface soil, planted squash, eggplant, corn.
I weeded, picked, peeled, chopped, sautéed in butter.
I sat down and ate with friends.

My hands grew tired, too sore to work the soil.
My heart grew weak, too wise to run in fear.

So I let the wind bend the weeds as the fire-wheels
and tickseeds bloomed. I watched the purple primrose
spread, as wild onions rose, covering their pungent heads.

I let the seeds burrow underground to survive
the summer heat, trusting they would crack
their tiny torsos, push their thin stems
through the ground.

But only when the time was right.

PART THREE: FOSSIL WINGS

Axis Ballroom

Everyone is here tonight.
Even the ring-tailed cat shining two
gold moons through the chinaberry tree.

The garter snake slips through the Calla Lilles
chewing on details I've let slide, like aphids
burrowed down in the coiled new leaves.

A lumbering coon rattles up the downspout.
Autumn's first cold snap is blowing in, and
she plans to squeeze through the air vent and
raise her family in the attic. Who can blame her?

All stayed home and kept things running
as I was off dealing with people,
their loud clamorings, their life, and death.

I now glaze my flashlight across the gray thicket
of trees to light upon the grand ballroom.
Dozens of tiny couples are suspended
awaiting the violins.

Part Three: Fossil Wings

Fossil Wings

We are always at some stage of burning.
A pine tree bursts into flame,
spitting its serotinous seed
to rise from black ash.

Or ice sheets crust
as oceans spin through time.

Let fires scald and blizzards stall you.
Every dying will be stamped in clay.

You've only to regard your world
as wind turns pages of the past,
and water tumbles stone.

The universe never sleeps.
It reimagines buried things.
It solders steel with bone
to make your wings.

BEVERLY BLATNER BAGELMAN was born and raised in Texas. She received her BBA from the University of Texas and her M.Ed. in Counseling from Texas State. As a psychotherapist in private practice, Beverly specialized in Dialectical Behavior Therapy, a skills-based modality that includes mindfulness and is designed to help individuals improve their ability to regulate intense emotions. After retiring in 2015, Beverly moved with her husband to the lake, where she enjoys spending time with her grandchildren Foster and Felicity, and her dog and cat, Puki and Sonnet. When she is not helping with an ambitious remodeling project, she is reading, writing, traveling, and always learning about poetry. Beverly was Shortlisted for the Raw Art Review Chapbook Poetry Prize through Uncollected Press and was the Winner of the 2017 Animal Passion Award through Austin Poetry Society. She's been published in Best Austin Poetry and Ocotillo Review. She hopes that these poems provide her readers with solid artifacts of meaning and hope.

www.ingramcontent.com/pod-product-compliance
Lightning Source LLC
Chambersburg PA
CBHW031819110426
42743CB00057B/993